A NOTE TO PARENTS

When your children are ready to ing them the right books—and lo. as giving them the right food to eat. **Step into Reading Books** present exciting stories or information reinforced with lively, colorful illustrations that make learning to read fun, satisfying, and worthwhile. They are priced so that acquiring an entire library of them is affordable. And they are beginning readers with an important difference—they're written on three levels.

Step 1 Books, with their very large type and extremely simple vocabulary, have been created for the very youngest readers. **Step 2 Books** are both longer and slightly more difficult. **Step 3 Books,** written to mid-second-grade reading levels, are for the child who has acquired even greater reading skills.

Children develop at different ages. **Step into Reading Books,** with their three levels of reading, are designed to help children become good—and interested—readers *faster.* The grade levels assigned to the three steps—preschool through grade 1 for Step 1, grades 1 through 3 for Step 2, and grades 2 and 3 for Step 3—are intended only as guides. Some children move through all three steps very rapidly; others climb the steps over a period of several years. These books will help your child "step into reading" in style!

For John and Jamie
—H.Z.

For Eric and Louie,
hungry for life
—C.N.

Library of Congress Cataloging-in-Publication Data:
Ziefert, Harriet. So hungry! (Step into reading. A Step 1 book) SUMMARY: Finding themselves extremely hungry, Lewis and Kate have fun making enormous sandwiches and eating them as fast as possible. [1. Sandwiches—Fiction. 2. Food habits—Fiction] I. Nicklaus, Carol, ill. II. Title. III. Series: Step into reading. Step 1 book. PZ7.Z487Sm 1987 [E] 87-4763 ISBN: 0-394-89127-9 (trade); 0-394-99127-3 (lib. bdg.)

Manufactured in the United States of America   1 2 3 4 5 6 7 8 9 0

STEP INTO READING is a trademark of Random House, Inc.

Step into Reading

SO HUNGRY!

by Harriet Ziefert and Carol Nicklaus

A Step 1 Book

Random House  New York

"I'm hungry," said Lewis.
"So hungry!"

"I'm hungry too,"
said Kate.

"Let's have cookies,"
said Kate.

"Good idea,"
said Lewis.

But there were no cookies
in the cookie jar.

No cookies
on the shelf.

And no cookies
in the refrigerator.

"I'm so hungry," said Kate.
"So, so hungry!" said Lewis.

"Here's some bread," said Kate.
"Let's make sandwiches."

"Great big sandwiches,"
said Lewis.

Kate said,
"I'll get the meat
and the cheese
and the lettuce."

Lewis said,

"I'll get the ketchup."

"I know how to make
a great sandwich,"
said Kate.
"Ketchup first...

Then cheese.

Then meat.

Then lettuce."

"I can make
    a better sandwich," said Lewis.
"Ketchup first...

Then cheese.

Then meat.''

"Then more cheese.
More meat.
More ketchup," Lewis said.

"This is a great sandwich,"
he said.
"A great big sandwich!"

"Mine is better than yours,"
said Kate.
"It has lettuce!"

22

"Mine is bigger than yours,"
said Lewis.
"It has double meat,
double cheese,
and double ketchup!"

"I bet I can eat mine faster," said Lewis.

"I bet you can't,"
said Kate.

"I bet I can take
  bigger bites," said Lewis.

"I bet you can't,"
said Kate.

"I'm done," said Lewis.
"Me too," said Kate.

Lewis burped.

Burp! Burp!

"Excuse me!" said Lewis.

"I'm not so hungry,"
said Lewis.

"I'm full," said Kate.

"So full!" said Lewis.